LIFE OF JESUS SERIES

TEACHINGS OF JESUS

Steven B. Borst

CONCORDIA PUBLISHING HOUSE · SAINT LOUIS

Edited by Thomas J. Doyle

This publication may be available in Braille, in large print, or on cassette tape for the visually impaired. Please allow 8 to 12 weeks for delivery. Write to Lutheran Braille Workers, P.O. Box 5000, Yucaipa, CA 92399; call toll-free 1-800-925-6092; or visit the website: www.LBWinc.org.

Song lyric on p. 11 from "In the Light" by Charles Peacock © 1995 Sparrow Song (BMI). Used by permission.

Excerpt on p. 14 from THE SECRET OF LOVING by Josh McDowell.© 1985 Here's Life Publishers, Inc. Used by permission of Tyndale House Publishers, Inc. All rights reserved.

Poem on p. 33 "The Road Not Taken" from THE POETRY OF ROBERT FROST edited by Edward Connery Lathem Copyright 1916, © 1969 by Henry Holt and Company, copyright 1944 by Robert Frost. Reprinted by permission of Henry Holt and Company, LLC.

Scripture quotations are taken from the HOLY BIBLE: NEW INTERNATIONAL VERSION® NIV®. Copyright © 1973, 1978, 1984 by International Bible Society. Used by permission of Zondervan Publishing House. All rights reserved.

Copyright © 2000 Concordia Publishing House 3558 S. Jefferson Avenue, St. Louis, MO 63118-3968

Manufactured in the United States of America

8   9   10   11   12   13   14   15   16   26   25   24   23   22   21   20   19   18

CONTENTS

Leaders Guide

INTRODUCTION

Life of Jesus explores the ministry and teachings of Jesus. Each study in this series includes 12 sessions addressing topics related to the study's theme. Life of Jesus gives Christians the opportunity to get "up close and personal" with the person and work of Jesus as they study God's Word and discuss applications to their lives with other Christians.

Life of Jesus uses a simple, user-friendly format consisting of four major components: Focus, Inform, Connect, and Vision.

Focus — introduces the participants to the concepts that will be explored during the session.

Inform — guides participants into Scripture to learn what God says about different issues.

Connect — provides activities and questions to help participants apply the truths found in Scripture to their lives.

Vision — suggests activities for additional growth during the week to come.

Life of Jesus can be used with large Bible study groups, in small groups, and by individuals as they seek to enrich their devotional life.

The accompanying Leaders Guide provides a suggested format for study and answers to questions.

May God strengthen you in the faith as you study His Word using Life of Jesus.

Session 1

PASS THE SALT: LIVING A BLESSED LIFE

FOCUS

Theologian Martin Franzmann says this about Jesus' Sermon on the Mount: "The Sermon on the Mount is the record of how Jesus moulds the will of His disciple, leading the disciple to live a life wholly drawn from God the King as He is revealed in these last days in His Son, a life which is therefore wholly lived for God the King. The gift of the Kingdom and the claim of the Kingdom (the call to repentance) are to shape the disciple's whole existence" (*Concordia Self-Study Commentary* [St. Louis: Concordia, 1979], 18).

As we spend the next 12 sessions looking at Jesus' words in Matthew 5–7, we will quickly become aware that Jesus' teaching is dynamically different from the world's. To His hearers, His teaching was also amazingly different from what they were taught by the religious leaders of their day. All who encounter Jesus' words, in whatever century, continent, or context, will find them refreshing, sometimes radical, and always challenging. In the sessions that follow, Jesus' teaching will challenge us anew about what it means to be righteous and faithful, as we live a life of love in true Christian piety.

The opening of Jesus' sermon sets a sort of electric atmosphere in the classroom of His hillside. He cuts to the very heart of the meaning of our existence as He describes what it means to lead a blessed life.

1. What does the world consider a "blessed person"?

2. Do you consider your life to be blessed? Why or why not?

INFORM

When Jesus uses the word *blessed*, he is speaking of God's gracious acts in our lives. God's most significant blessing is His Son, Jesus Christ. Those who sat at His feet that day, as well as we who sit in our classrooms or living rooms right now, are blessed to receive Christ and His teaching!

1. Read Matthew 5:1–12. In verses 3 and 4, Jesus describes people who realize and confess their inadequacy and sinfulness. Why would they be blessed?

2. The world says the powerful will inherit the earth. How and why does Jesus contradict people who believe this?

3. How will a blessed person react to others' misdeeds (v. 7)?

4. "Those who hunger and thirst for righteousness" and those who are "pure in heart" are people who have a single devotion to God. How does Jesus enlighten our understanding of the First Commandment with these words? Remember the First Commandment: "You shall have no other gods."

5. Verses 10–12 flatly contradict what we normally hope for in order to "rejoice and be glad" in our daily life. What does Jesus teach us about being His disciples? What promises of blessing does He give us?

Read Matthew 5:13–16.

1. In this section, Jesus describes how blessed people of God can be a blessing to the world. Why does Jesus call us salt?

2. What does it mean to be the "light of the world"? For whose glory are our blessed acts done?

CONNECT

Psalm 32:1–7 further defines the blessed person. Read these verses and connect them to your own life by answering the following questions.

1. The world places a high commodity on being strong, not showing weakness, and always being right. How much does this mind-set affect your personal and professional life? How can you identify with the psalmist in verses 3–4?

2. Verse 1 says that the truly blessed person is one who has experienced the forgiveness of sins through Christ's death on the cross. Look back to your answer for question 2 in the "Focus" section. How does this basic principle affect your own view of blessedness?

3. How have you experienced the blessing of God being your shelter during a crisis of "rising waters" (v. 6)?

VISION

At dinner this week, light a candle and make sure a saltshaker is on the table. Let these be a reminder to you and your family that God has blessed you through Jesus, and that Jesus is now sending you out as seasoning and light into a tasteless, dark world. In your prayers, ask the Lord for faith to see yourself as completely blessed and for wisdom in how to bring glory to God through blessed acts.

Session 2

HEY DIDDLE, DIDDLE; EVERY JOT AND TITTLE!

FOCUS

Have you seen those mazes on TV that Midwestern farmers have created in the midst of their huge cornfields? I had always been skeptical about the difficulty of these mazes and wondered if they offered any entertainment value whatsoever. I doubted so . . . until I tried one myself. The first large maze I lost myself in (literally!) was not in the Midwest, but in Hawaii. I participated in the maze created by the Dole Plantation, which, as you can probably guess, is in the shape of a pineapple.

The task was simple enough: we had to find six stations within the maze. At each station was a stencil of a picture, which we were to trace on our official entry form. The quickest time of the day would win some prize provided by Dole. My theory was that your love of pineapple juice directly corresponded to how eager you were to set the fastest time of the day. Since I think pineapples are an acquired taste, I was happy enough to try to come out somewhere in the middle of the pack.

The first two stations were simple enough. Even by silly luck, one could find a station merely by listening to the yells of the children and teenagers who had gone before you. Finding the rest of the stations, however, took more discipline. Though I firmly believed my superior use of reasoning and direction would whisk me through the maze in short order, I was soon humbled to learn that I wasn't any different from the others running in circles within the maze. I experienced wrong turns, paths that looked vaguely familiar, and complete loss of perspective. (In retrospect, I should have used the ET, Reese's Pieces method!) I finally made it out of the maze some 45 minutes later—a full 27 minutes behind the best time of the day—fully frustrated.

Life can be similar to a maze, can't it? Do you ever feel like you're not making any progress? Is your life fraught with a number of wrong turns? Is it easy to lose your perspective? Describe a time in your life when you felt like you were lost in a maze, and share it with the rest of the group.

INFORM

By the time Jesus started His public ministry, the religious elite of Judaism, many generations of scholars, had produced an extensive code of ethics and laws. What had started out as the Ten Commandments at Mt. Sinai was now an elaborate system of what to do and what not to do to be truly faithful. It was like being caught in a legal maze, and most people were constantly afraid of making a wrong turn.

This type of codification of God's Law often led to hypocrisy and shallow ritualism. (Jesus points this out on numerous occasions in the Gospels.) In His Sermon on the Mount, Jesus teaches a true interpretation of God's will for our lives. Read Matthew 5:17–20 and see how He introduces this topic.

1. What does Jesus say about the endurance of God's Law (v. 18)?

2. What does Jesus say about the severity of breaking God's Law (v. 19)?

3. What kind of hope does He give the average Israelite in regard to the person's own righteousness (v. 20)?

4. When it comes to the Law, what is Jesus' mission on our behalf (v. 17)?

CONNECT

1. Do you often have a guilty conscience? Are you constantly aware of your failure to fulfill God's Law? Where would you place yourself on the scale below?

constantly aware of my guilt   never feel regret

Read John 19:16–22, 28–30.

2. Jesus is the One who has fulfilled the Law for us. He is the One whose righteousness surpasses that of the Pharisees! Through faith, Christ's righteousness completely covers you, and you are seen as holy in the Father's eyes. How easy or difficult is it for you to accept yourself as God accepts you?

VISION

The lyrics of the song "In the Light" go like this:

> I keep trying to find a life
> On my own, apart from you.
> I am the king of excuses.
> I've got one for every selfish thing I do.
> *Chorus:*
> What's going on inside of me?
> I despise my own behavior.
> This only serves to confirm my suspicions
> That I'm still a man in need of a Savior.

(Charlie Peacock, "In the Light." On the compact disc *Jesus Freak*. Performed by dc Talk. Additional lyrics by Toby McKeehan.)

Learn to seek Christ's righteousness. Through Him you are made right with God and will be empowered to better live out that righteousness in your life. In your prayers this week, include this petition: "Lord Jesus, I thank You for fulfilling all righteousness for me on the cross and for making me holy. By Your Holy Spirit, may I live a life that mirrors Your righteous life."

Session 3

MURDER HE RE-WROTE

FOCUS

As His sermon continues, Jesus begins to get more specific about every "jot and tittle" of the Law. As He does so, He completely deflates those who would claim to be righteous by their own acts. Even the Pharisees, who boasted of keeping the letter of the Law, could in no way keep the heart of the Law. At the same time, Jesus shows those who have received His righteousness what it means to lead a life of faith and love.

In this section of His sermon, Jesus deals with the Fifth Commandment: "You shall not murder." Write your definition of murder.

INFORM

Read Matthew 5:21–26.

    1. How does Jesus expand the definition of murder in verses 21–22?

    2. Murder is born from an angry heart. For those who want to be judged by the Law, what consequences result when anger lashes out, whether with weapons or words?

    3. Instead of anger and murder, what does this commandment tell us God desires between feuding parties (vv. 23–26)?

Read 1 John 3:11–16.

    1. Of what murder does John remind us (vv. 11–12)? What caused this murder?

    2. How does John connect hate with murder (vv. 13–15)?

3. Jesus allowed Himself to be murdered for our sake. What response does this cause in us (v. 16)?

CONNECT

God desires us to be reconciled not just with Him, but with our brothers and sisters as well. Later in the Gospel of Matthew, Jesus describes exactly what it means to "leave your gift there in front of the altar . . . and be reconciled." Read Matthew 18:15–20, and connect these verses to your life.

1. What wisdom is there in Jesus' method?

2. When you are wronged, how often do you privately go and show that person his or her fault?

3. Jesus describes how we work for reconciliation not just once, but a number of times, and with a number of resources. When have you seen such a method used? How did it work?

4. Jesus completely redefines murder. Look back at your definition in the "Focus" section of this chapter. Having studied Jesus' teaching, write a new definition.

VISION

Jesus has reconciled you to the Father by offering His life on the cross for your sins. Rejoice in God's forgiveness. Let that forgiveness take root and flower in your life by striving for such reconciliation with others. Write the name of someone with whom you need to be reconciled below. Make contact with him or her this week! Begin the process of reconciliation.

Session 4

HOLY VOW! KEEPING YOUR WORD AND BEING FAITHFUL

FOCUS

Josh McDowell, in his book *The Secret of Loving* (Wheaton, Illinois: Tyndale, 1988), says this about marital commitment:

> What kind of commitment did you build into your marriage vows? Did you include "until death do us part"? If you did, you are in a minority. Commitment is hardly a buzzword these days. . . . I have come to believe that most couples are defeated even before they marry. They enter into marriage with the attitude, "If it doesn't work, or if we have problems, we will simply dispose of it." This shallow view of commitment is best described by the phrases "out of sight, out of mind" and "if you're not with the one you love, love the one you're with." (pp. 309–10.)

1. Describe the marital commitment of your parents, grandparents, aunts, and uncles when you were a child.

2. How did their commitment (or lack thereof) affect you as you grew up?

INFORM

Read Matthew 5:27–32.

1. What does Jesus teach about the heart of the Sixth Commandment in verses 27–28?

2. What does Jesus mean when He suggests radical surgery for those tempted by adulterous thoughts?

3. How seriously does God take marriage (vv. 31–32)?

4. What allowances does God give, even though divorce is contrary to His will (v. 32)?

Read Matthew 5:33–37.

1. Why do you think Jesus includes this section right after His teaching on marriage?

2. What does this section say about the integrity of our word?

CONNECT

Jesus uses vivid language ("gouge" and "cut it off") when it comes to fleeing fornication. While we would never dream of taking Christ's words literally, Christ experienced such pain in His own body when He died for our sins on the cross. Read Romans 6:1–14 and then answer the following questions.

1. St. Paul makes a strong connection between Christ's crucifixion and our Baptism into His death. Sexual sins often carry with them a personal shame that isn't easy to forget. Have you truly experienced the complete forgiveness of Christ for your lustful thoughts and inappropriate sexual expressions?

2. Not only did we receive Christ's death for forgiveness, but we've also been raised with Him to new life. What is one way in which you can practically apply verse 12 in your life?

VISION

This week, carefully observe your promises. Examine the trustworthiness of your word. If you are married, watch your wedding video or look through your wedding album with your spouse, and renew your vows to one another. In all of these activities, be strengthened in the knowledge that God keeps His promises of love, mercy, and forgiveness to you!

Session 5

WHAT AN EXTRAORDINARY LOVE!

FOCUS

For over 30 years, apartheid ruled South Africa. Black Africans were stripped of many basic human rights. Countless beatings, imprisonments, tortures, and killings occurred at the hands of the ruling, white minority. But when civil rights leader Nelson Mandela was released after decades of imprisonment, he spearheaded an effort to overthrow apartheid and became the first nationally elected president.

What shocked the world was how Mandela's government dealt with its enemies: South Africa set up Truth and Reconciliation Commission. This commission had three committees. The Human Rights Violations Committee investigated any human rights abuses that took place between 1960 and 1994. The findings of this committee were then sent to the Reparation and Rehabilitation Committee, whose chief responsibility was to restore victims' dignity and offer rehabilitation and healing to survivors, their families, and communities at large. The third committee initially drew the most attention. The Amnesty Commitee allowed perpetrators to "apply for amnesty for any act, omission or offence associated with a political objective." To make their aim absolutely clear, this committee stated "Being granted amnesty for an act means that the perpetrator is free from prosecution for that particular act."

(Information taken from the official Web page for the Truth and Reconciliation Commission:www.truth.org.za. Direct quotes can be found on the home page.)

1. Place yourself as a black South African in 1995. Your family experienced personal injustice. How would you react to the announcement of the amnesty process? Why?

2. Now place yourself in the shoes of a white minority politician. For certain acts, whether violent, judicial, or political, you could be indicted for crimes against humanity. Would you apply for amnesty, face your victims, and plead for forgiveness? How easy or difficult is the offer of amnesty to accept?

INFORM

Read Matthew 5:38–42.

1. Jesus suggests that we ought to leave the law of justice and retribution with God and His instruments for civil peace—government. The disciple is to respond to the "evil person" with love. What three examples does Jesus give in verses 39–41 for how we might do this?

16

2. Which one of these examples seems the most difficult love response? Why?

3. In verse 42, Jesus shifts our focus slightly: we move from being ordered to being asked. How does our response of love look to those in need?

Read Matthew 5:43–48.

1. Jesus once again quotes the Old Testament Law and contrasts it with the way of grace and love. How does He desire we treat our enemies? Why does Jesus connect this with our being children of God?

2. How does God treat His enemies (v. 45)?

3. Discuss how Jesus differentiates between the world's love and God's extraordinary love in verses 46–47.

4. How does verse 48 connect love with holiness?

Read Romans 12:9–21.

1. This passage begins, "Love must be sincere." How do verses 9–16 describe sincere love?

2. What is the plea of verse 18? What hard reality does it address? What responsibility does it put on disciples of Christ?

3. Some might think that this teaching of an extraordinary love is irresponsible because it seems to completely gloss over evil acts. How does verse 19 contradict this notion?

4. Reread verse 21. What greater power do Christians have in fighting evil?

CONNECT

The extraordinary love that Jesus describes to His disciples is the very love that God has poured out on us. Romans 5:8 tells us: "But God demonstrates His own love for us in this: While we were still sinners, Christ died for us." Even though we were God's enemies because of our rebellion and sin, Jesus died for us. He loved us before we ever repented or believed in Him. He loved us while we were still His enemies. You can say, then, that Jesus is our "truth and reconciliation"! Through Him, we have become reconciled to God and changed from God's foes to God's friends.

Read Luke 23:32–34, and connect Christ's words to your life as you answer the following questions.

1. Have you experienced the extraordinary love of God in your life?

2. Think of a person you know who concretely overcame evil with good. How have you witnessed this to be true?

3. Grade yourself (A, B, C, D, or F) on how well you have loved your enemies as Christ has loved you. If you gave yourself less than a B, why in particular is it difficult for you to forgive them?

VISION

Jesus instructs us to love our enemies and to pray for them. In your prayers this week, include the following:

1. Identify someone with whom you are at odds. Pray that God would help you to be confident in His love for you so that you might boldly show love to this particular person.

2. Pray for a heart to forgive and the courage to communicate forgiveness to this person.

3. Walter Wangerin Jr. describes God's extraordinary love as "divine absurdity"; only God could love like that! He reminds us that "the sin against you was also a personal sin against God. . . . The gravest consequence of sin, then, is not what you suffer, but what [the one who sinned against you] might suffer" (*As for Me and My House* [Nashville: Thomas Nelson, 1987], 98). Pray that your enemy would be reconciled not only to you, but to God.

Session 6
HYPOCRITE!

FOCUS

The word *hypocrite* has been around for a long time. It is, in fact, a direct transliteration of the classical Greek word *hypokrites*. What did hypokrites originally mean? You might be surprised to find out that it didn't have a negative connotation. Hypokrites meant "actor." It was the word used to describe not only those on the stage, but also people who read poetry or gave speeches.

It's easy to see how hypokrites evolved into the meaning we use today. When we call somebody a hypocrite, we are implying that they are acting out a part. Hypocrites boast of their morality and accomplishments, but in fact they are not truly who they claim to be.

1. What professions (other than acting!) have a reputation of having a high percentage of hypocrites? Do you agree with this bad rap? Why or why not?

2. In what area of your life could you be accused of being a hypocrite? Why?

INFORM

In Matthew 6, Jesus' sermon shifts from exhorting us to have extraordinary love to decrying outlandish hypocrisy. Jesus particularly points out how this hypocrisy is shown in giving, praying, and fasting. Read the following sections of Scripture and answer the questions relating to them.

Read Matthew 6:1–4.

1. What motivates people to do "acts of righteousness" to be seen by men?

2. Describe the outlandish hypocrisy Jesus denounces in verse 2.

3. Summarize verse 3 in your own words. What is the motivation of someone who gives in this way?

Read Matthew 6:5–8.

1. How do hypocrites pray? How do pagans pray?

2. In what setting does Jesus urge us to pray?

3. What comfort does Jesus provide in verse 8?

Read Matthew 6:16–18.

1. In verse 16 Jesus uses a phrase for the third time: "I tell you the truth, they have received their reward in full." What does He mean by it?

2. What purpose does Jesus give in verse 18 for washing our faces when we fast?

3. Jesus uses another phrase for the third time at the end of verse 18: "Your Father, who sees what is done in secret, will reward you." What does Jesus mean by this?

CONNECT

Jesus gives a more complete discourse on the hypocrisy of the church and its leaders in Matthew 23. Skim the seven woes in verses 13, 15, 16, 23, 25, 27, and 29. Then answer the following questions.

1. Using no more than three words for every "woe," describe the seven woes.

2. Out of the seven, which one do you think could serve as a warning for the church today?

3. If you had to craft a list entitled "The Seven Hypocrisies in My Life," what seven would make the list?

Read Romans 7:21–25a.

1. How does St. Paul describe his struggle with hypocrisy? Do you identify with his struggle? Why or why not?

2. Jesus is the Healer of hypocrisy. How is Jesus the exact opposite of hypokrites? How did Jesus rescue us from our bodies of death?

VISION

Jesus was laid in the tomb so that we, who are like whitewashed tombs, might be cleansed on the inside. Jesus, who is the Truth, can rescue us who so easily fall into hypocrisy. Consider the following actions as you are empowered by Jesus' rescue of you from hypocrisy and all other sin by His death on the cross.

1. Take off your actor's mask in the presence of God. Come clean with the Father, and through Christ, He will forgive you!

2. Pray about your answer to question 2 in the "Focus" section. Determine how you might take three concrete steps to improve in this area. Write these steps below and ask for the Holy Spirit's strength to carry them out.

Session 7

LET US PRAY

FOCUS

In the last session, we studied Jesus' teaching about our "acts of righteousness" before people. Jesus taught us to refrain from publicly uttering beautifully ornate prayers for the sole purpose of impressing those who hear us. Jesus tells us how not to pray and then gives us a concrete example of how we can pray. As we begin to examine this topic, evaluate your own prayer life by answering the following questions.

1. Where is your favorite place to pray? Why?

2. Place an X on both scales below to describe your typical prayer:

short/sweet	long/drawn–out
intense/emotional	quiet/meditative

INFORM

Read Matthew 6:9–13.

1. How does Jesus teach us to address God in our prayers? How does Jesus balance this intimacy with the last phrase of verse 9?

2. Verse 10 concerns itself with God's affairs. For what exactly do we pray in this verse?

3. Martin Luther writes that "daily bread" in verse 11 consists of "everything that has to do with the support and needs of the body" (*Luther's Small Catechism with Explanation*, [St. Louis: Concordia, 1986], p. 18). How does Jesus teaching us to pray about such things comfort us?

4. From the earthly things of bread and sins, Jesus moves us to pray about what spiritual things in verses 12–13?

Read Matthew 6:14–15.

1. What does Jesus teach us, as people who have received God's forgiveness, about forgiving those who sin against us?

2. It almost sounds as if Jesus makes our forgiveness something we earn by first forgiving others. How do we rightly understand these verses in the context of the forgiveness Jesus won for us on the cross?

CONNECT

1. The Lord's Prayer is a valuable gift to Christians because it gives us a pattern by which to formulate our prayers. The Lord's Prayer teaches us to pray first about "God things" (His name, His kingdom, and His will) and then about "human things" (bread, forgiveness, temptation, and evil). Do your own prayers reflect this outline? If not, what pattern do your prayers follow?

2. Read Hebrews 10:19–23. Why can we confidently approach God's throne in prayer? How can you be sure your prayers are acceptable to God?

3. Read Romans 8:15–16, 26–27. What promise does God give, even when we don't know what to pray? What reassurance do these verses give you, especially when you try to pray for God's will?

VISION

Dietrich Bonhoeffer, a German pastor executed by the Nazis in 1945, wrote about the power of prayer. Through his experiences, he came to value the Book of Psalms as a book of prayer. Bonhoeffer wrote, "In the Psalter we learn to pray on the basis of Christ's prayer. The Psalter is the great school of prayer" (*Life Together* [San Francisco: Harper & Row, 1954], 47). In other words, through the Psalms we learn the magnitude of the Lord's Prayer.

Use the Psalms in your devotional life. Learn from them how to pray. Recite the Lord's Prayer for your own prayers. Finally, be confident in your prayers, for no matter how long or short, eloquent or stumbling, your prayers are acceptable to the Father through Jesus, in whose name you pray.

Session 8

Show Me the Treasure!

FOCUS

Imagine for a moment that you are driving home from work one day, and as you pull up in your driveway, you find two armed militiamen waiting for you at your front door. They coolly inform you that there has been a violent takeover of your city and that you have 10 minutes to gather some personal things and leave. Within your home is all you possess in the world: furniture, books, jewelry, pictures, official documents, and an ATM card to access all your cash. You have no time to deliberate on what you should pack. You must instead decide on instinct. What seems most important to you on a "gut level"? Your task, in the next 30 seconds, is to list the top five things you would take. Ready? Go!

1.
2.
3.
4.
5.

INFORM

Read Jesus' instructions about our treasures in Matthew 6:19–24.

1. How does Jesus differentiate between earthly and heavenly treasures in verses 19–20?

2. According to verse 21, how does wealth affect our priorities?

3. Verses 22–23 switch our focus from the heart to the eyes. How does what we seek after in life affect our very being? Do you think we realize it when we fill our bodies with "darkness"?

4. In verse 24, Jesus draws a line in the sand. How would you describe His message?

   In the Book of Revelation, God instructs St. John to write His prophetic

Word to seven churches in Asia Minor. One of these churches, Laodicea (lay-ah-di-see-ah), struggled with trying to serve two masters. Read the letter to them in Revelation 3:14–18.

1. How is their spirituality described in verses 15–16?

2. How have they deceived themselves (v. 17)?

3. What is God's counsel in verse 18? What does God mean by "gold," "white clothes," and "salve"?

CONNECT

Would your life be described as "Laodicean"? Are you trying to juggle serving two masters? If so, listen to the advice St. Paul gives young Timothy in 1 Timothy 6:17–19, and apply it to your life.

1. We are not to be arrogant about what we have, nor are we to put our hope in these possessions. With which of these two values do you struggle most? Why?

2. God provides everything for our enjoyment. He has given us the most precious treasure, Jesus Christ, who died for our debts on the cross. We are debt-free people, having our "sin bill" paid in full by Jesus' crucifixion. How do God's gifts, both spiritual and temporal, make you a wealthy person? How are you rich in Christ?

3. What does verse 18 say we are to do with our wealth? What is one practical way you can be "rich in good deeds"?

VISION

For many, the scenario included in the "Focus" section is not that unusual. Many people throughout the world have had to make these sorts of decisions. Closer to home, we are all vulnerable to losing what we have in an instant—whether through fire, flood, or a crash in the stock market. That's why St. Paul tells us not to put our "hope in wealth, which is so uncertain."

Show me the treasure! Jesus' words, "For where your treasure is, there your heart will be also," are true! God can change your heart by His treasures of forgiveness and faith. He will calm your anxiety through His real presence in the Lord's Supper. He provides you daily with all that you need to support your life.

Ironically, our natural instinct to hoard our wealth and spend it on ourselves causes us to become slaves to our earthly wealth. Christ, who gave His life for us, teaches us to give our lives to others. How can we be rich in good works? How can we break free from the service of self? It is when we begin to give our God-given wealth away to others that we share our treasures of forgiveness, love, food, and drink with those around us, and that we, through faith, serve God as our Master.

Session 9

STRESS LESS!

FOCUS

It's easy to recognize the signs: a tense back, a strained neck, a clenched jaw. You're biting your nails, your stomach is churning, and you have a headache between the eyes. These are all sure signs of stress. While it is easy to recognize these symptoms, once they are set into motion, it's rather difficult to stop them.

Consider the level of stress you experienced this past week. Then answer the following questions.

1. Place an *X* on the scale below to indicate what best describes you this past week.

happy-go-lucky   even-keeled   a flurry of worry

2. What was the number one thing that stressed you this past week? Have you found any resolution to your worries? Why or why not?

INFORM

As Jesus continues His Sermon on the Mount, He comes to us in the midst of our stress-filled lives and proclaims a simple dictum: "stress less!" Read His words in Matthew 6:25–34.

In this section, Jesus gives us seven reasons to stop worrying. Write down the corresponding reason next to the verses below.

1.   Verse 25:

2.   Verse 26:

3.   Verse 27:

4.   Verses 28–30:

5.   Verses 31–32:

6.   Verse 33:

7.   Verse 34:

During His ministry, Jesus sent out the 12 disciples into Israel, proclaiming the Gospel and healing the sick in His name. Read part of Jesus' send-off speech in Matthew 10:5–30.

1. In verses 8–16, what directives does Jesus give the disciples regarding food, clothing, money, and shelter? Why do you suppose He sent them out with these instructions?

2. What stress does Jesus conquer in verses 17–20?

3. What comforting words does Jesus give His anxious disciples in verses 29–31?

CONNECT

Stress is a trumpet call for our body to move into action. However, instead of trying to do something productive in our alerted state, we too often spend our energy worrying. In Philippians 4:6–8, we are given guidelines on how to handle stress. Read this section and then connect it to your own circumstances as you answer the questions.

1. St. Paul, who wrote this section, suggests that instead of allowing ourselves to be swallowed up by anxiety, we can actually do something proactive: pray! Look back at your biggest stress during the past week (this was your answer to "Focus" question 2). Have you committed it to prayer? Why or why not?

2. St. Paul adds an important phrase to the activity of prayer: "with thanksgiving." So often when we stress over life's problems, we lose our perspective. Despite those things you are worrying about right now, for what things are you thankful? Can our "thanksgiving list" dwarf our "complaint list"?

3. Verse 8 suggests alternative things on which to set our thoughts. When you are facing a stressful situation, what is one true, noble, just, pure, and lovely thing on which you can dwell?

VISION

So what does Jesus teach about stressing over earthly things? "Seek first His kingdom and His righteousness, and all these things will be given to you as well." Jesus took care of our biggest stresses in life! Through His death on the cross, Jesus has destroyed death, paid for our sin, and conquered the power of the devil. We are free and forgiven people, and God is faithful in loving and keeping us in His grace! He who gave up His Son for our salvation will also provide us with "all these things" we need in life.

This week, be proactive when stress sets in. Spend time in prayer. Find ways to enter into "thanks living." Memorize one of the verses from the list of seven reasons to stop worrying that you filled out in the "Inform" section, and recite it when you feel overwhelmed. Because God is good, we can indeed stress less!

A Visine Cure for Judging Others

FOCUS

It was a Wednesday morning in December as I sat as juror number seven in a small deliberation room with 11 new acquaintances. We had listened to two days of testimony regarding a prison inmate accused of bringing illegal contraband into the penitentiary via the mail. Someone on the outside had fabricated legal papers to be sent to him, and thus his package arrived as legal mail. Regular mail is opened and searched by the guards prior to being delivered to the inmates, but legal mail can only be opened in the presence of an inmate.

On the day in question, the guard brought the accused inmate his legal mail, and as the guard looked through the papers, he noticed two sheets glued together, with a small dark spot in the upper right-hand corner. As the guard began to examine these sheets more closely, the inmate reached through the bars of his cell, grabbed the papers from the officer, and began flushing parts of the package down the toilet. He was quickly pepper–sprayed and hauled out of his cell as the guards retrieved the remains of the package. There were several more sheets glued together that had dark spots between them too. The dark spots were later identified as small amounts of heroin.

As it turned out, the inmate incarcerated in the cell directly next to the accused was the kingpin of the so-called prison mafia. This mafia boss (who was sentenced to over 450 years) took the stand to say that it was he who ordered the drugs sent and that the accused had no prior knowledge of the delivery. The kingpin, of course, had nothing to lose in making this confession, because he would never be released from prison anyway.

As we drank really bad courthouse coffee, my fellow jurors and I reviewed the evidence. After a day of deliberating, we put together what we believed was the truth: the accused was forced by the mafia boss to receive the drugs. If he did as he was told, he would gain favor with the rulers of the mafia. If he refused, he would suffer their wrath. The accused had been put "between a rock and a hard place," but by the end of the day, we gave the only verdict we could give: "Guilty!" According to the law, the accused knew the drugs were going to be delivered to his cell, and he willingly took possession of them. After giving our verdict, we learned one more fact that had been withheld from us during the trial: this guilty decision was the accused's third strike. He would now never be free again.

That evening, I led an Advent service in my congregation. My day had started in a judicial setting that knew only of law and punishment. My day ended in the setting of God's house, where I was called to proclaim a message of love and forgiveness.

1. Have you ever had to judge someone strictly according to the rules, for instance, at work or at a sports event?

2. What was easy or difficult about that task? Why?

INFORM

In Matthew 7, Jesus delves into the personal judgments we make in our daily lives. Read Matthew 7:1–6.

1. What is Jesus' warning in verses 1–2?

2. What problem regarding judging others does Jesus point out in verse 3?

3. What admonition does Jesus give in verses 4–5?

Read Romans 14:1–3, 7–13.

1. Paul is addressing matters of conscience, or "disputable matters." How is it possible for two Christians to disagree on these matters and yet both be pleasing to God?

2. Who is the judge of our actions according to verses 3, 7–8?

3. What does Christ's death and resurrection have to do with this issue (see v. 9)?

4. In verse 13, what alternate action does Paul suggest we take?

CONNECT

When we judge others, we enter into the realm of law and punishment. Like the courtroom described at the beginning of this session, there is no room for mercy here. When we judge others, we place ourselves and our conduct into this graceless place as well. Yet our God of love earnestly desires to bring people who are crushed by the Law into His realm of grace and forgiveness.

1. Walter Wangerin says, "The sins we see easiest in others we learned first in ourselves" (*As for Me and My House* [Nashville: Thomas Nelson, 1987], 99). Do you agree or disagree? Why?

2. Jesus' "visine cure" for judgment is to first take the plank out of our own eye. This is done through confession and the forgiveness of sins. What particular plank needs to be removed from your eye?

3. Jesus doesn't tell Christians never to judge people's actions. Christ tells us, "First take the plank out of your own eye, and then you will see clearly to remove the speck from your brother's eye." In other words, when we confront others, we need to realize that we are just as reliant on God's grace as they are. How can you judge someone's actions in the spirit that Jesus describes?

VISION

Because Christ died on the planks of the cross, we can have the planks in our eyes removed. With renewed vision, we can begin to help others who are caught in the struggle of sin to step out of judgment and into God's realm of grace. Take these words of James 1:19–21 to heart: "My dear brothers, take note of this: Everyone should be quick to listen, slow to speak and slow to become angry, for man's anger does not bring about the righteous life that God desires. Therefore, get rid of all moral filth and the evil that is so prevalent and humbly accept the word planted in you, which can save you."

Session 11

FOLLOW THE NARROW BRICK ROAD

FOCUS

Robert Frost, in his classic poem "The Road Not Taken," describes a dilemma he faced while walking in a yellow wood. The road upon which he was walking diverged, and he was forced to decide which path to take.

> *Two roads diverged in a yellow wood,*
> *And sorry I could not travel both*
> *And be one traveler, long I stood*
> *And looked down one as far as I could*
> *To where it bent in the undergrowth.*
>
> *Then took the other, as just as fair,*
> *And having perhaps the better claim,*
> *Because it was grassy and wanted wear;*
> *Though as for that the passing there*
> *Had worn them really about the same.*
>
> *And both that morning equally lay*
> *In leaves no step had trodden black.*
> *Oh, I kept the first for another day!*
> *Yet knowing how way leads on to way,*
> *I doubted if I should ever come back.*
>
> *I shall be telling this with a sigh*
> *Somewhere ages and ages hence:*
> *Two roads diverged in a wood, and I—*
> *I took the one less traveled by,*
> *and that has made all the difference.*

Describe a time in your life in which you reached a fork in the road. What were your options? How did you decide which option to choose? What path did you take? Did you make the right choice?

INFORM

Read Matthew 7:7–14.

1. When we are confused and don't know which path to take, Jesus tells us to ask, seek, and knock. In verse 8, what promises does Jesus give to those who go to Him?

2. How does Jesus compare God our Father to our earthly parents in verses 9–11?

3. Verse 12 is known as the Golden Rule. Describe the meaning of this verse in your own words.

4. Jesus tells us that the road of life diverges. How does He describe each path?

Read John 10:7–10.

1. What does Jesus call Himself in verse 7?

2. What promises does Jesus give for all who enter through Him?

CONNECT

Jesus Christ claims that He is the narrow gate to true and eternal life. No one can come to the Father except through faith in Him. Read Proverbs 3:5–6 and connect its message to your life.

1. We are not to lean "on our own understanding," but rather we are to ask, seek, and knock for the Lord's guidance. What is one issue or decision in your life for which you need greater spiritual understanding?

2. Psalm 119:105 says, "Your Word is a lamp to my feet and a light for my path." How would you grade yourself in going to God's Word for direction in your life?

3. God's promise is that He will make our paths straight. Looking back on your life, how has God guided you through a particularly difficult time?

VISION

Many people give us advice on which paths we should take. Talk shows, editorials, horoscopes, music, and movies all scream directions to choose a certain path. In the midst of this shouting match, Jesus comes with a clear voice and beckons us to seek Him. He gladly opens the doors of His goodness because He loves us, and He is eager to answer our prayers according to His will. In fact, Jesus gives us much more than good advice. Through His death on the cross for our sin, He has opened for us the narrow path that leads to eternal life. His words give us true direction, and they come with power and blessing.

Session 12

WHY DO WE KEEP FOOLING AROUND?

FOCUS

As we reach the end of Matthew 7, Jesus begins to "land" His sermon. He does this by describing the two types of people who have heard His preaching: the wise, who put Jesus' words into practice, and the fools, who do not follow Jesus' instruction. Before reading the conclusion of Jesus' Sermon on the Mount, attempt to differentiate between wisdom and foolishness by creating an acrostic out of the two words below. For each letter in the word *wise*, write a word that begins with that letter. Each of your four words should help describe a wise person. After you complete the first word, go on to describe a *fool* by writing a word for each of its letters.

W=   F=
I=   O=
S=   O=
E=   L=

INFORM

Read Matthew 7:15–28.

1. In verses 15–20, how does Jesus tell us we can recognize false prophets?

2. What sad reality does Jesus make plain in verses 21–28? What do these false disciples lack?

3. How does Jesus describe a wise person in verses 24–25? How does a strong foundation help as you face life's storms?

4. Jesus describes the fool as one who builds on sand. What kind of foolish building goes on most frequently in the lives of people you know?

5. When Jesus finally finishes His great sermon, what is the crowd's reaction?

Read Acts 4:5–12.

1. The Jewish leaders called Peter and John before them, because they had healed a crippled man in the temple. By whose authority did they do so?

2. How does Peter describe Jesus in verse 11? How does this serve as a foundation to verse 12?

CONNECT

The first nine chapters of Proverbs introduce the rest of the book and show the difference between wisdom and foolishness. Read Proverbs 4:1–9, and connect it to your life by answering the following questions.

1. In our modern world filled with information, how easy or difficult is it to distinguish between wisdom and foolishness?

2. Look at verse 7. How can you apply this verse to your life?

3. Jesus says, "Everyone who hears these words of Mine and puts them into practice is like a wise man who built his house on the rock." How can Jesus' wise words, especially His promises of forgiveness and grace, help you stand up under life's storms?

4. If you have worked on previous sessions in this Bible study guide, look back over some of the topics Jesus addressed in the Sermon on the Mount. Which particular session has been the most insightful for you? How can you begin to wisely put what you have learned into practice?

VISION

People came to Jesus and asked, "What must we do to do the works God requires?" Jesus answered them, "The work of God is this: to believe in the one He has sent" (John 6:28–29). In hearing Jesus preach about such topics as murder, adultery, divorce, giving to the needy, and prayer, we might get the impression that to be a true disciple of Jesus, we must first follow His instructions. Yet Jesus began His Sermon on the Mount by calling blessed all those who thirst and hunger for Him.

God has made you a disciple of Jesus by His grace through faith. Jesus gave His life on the cross for you as payment for all the times when you didn't live up to God's high standards. Cling to the wisdom of the Gospel with all your strength! It is then, as God's forgiven child, that you will be strengthened to wisely live your faith according to the radical teachings of Jesus in His Sermon on the Mount.

TEACHINGS OF JESUS

LEADERS GUIDE

Session 1

PASS THE SALT: LIVING A BLESSED LIFE

FOCUS

Read aloud or invite volunteers to read aloud the opening paragraph.

1. Answers will vary. The world often sees health and wealth as signs of a blessed life.

2. Answers will vary.

INFORM

Have a volunteer read aloud Matthew 5:1–12.

1. God offers grace and forgiveness to all who come to Him in humility and faith. Those who realize they are "poor in spirit" and who "mourn" over their inadequacies will, through Christ, be reconciled to God, and thus inherit the kingdom of heaven.

2. Jesus quite startlingly says that the meek, not the powerful, will inherit the earth. The whole world is God's, and He desires to bless those who in meekness call Him Lord.

3. Those who have received God's mercy will in turn be merciful to others.

4. The First Commandment states "You shall have no other gods." Those who have singleness of devotion to God truly worship Him alone.

5. Disciples of Christ expect insults and persecutions from the world. Although on the surface this does not seem anything over which to rejoice, Jesus reminds us that both He and the prophets faced the same persecution. We can rejoice because "the one who is in you is greater than the one who is in the world" (1 John 4:4). We will reap an eternity of God's blessings.

Have someone read aloud Matthew 5:13–16.

1. Salt serves two functions: it preserves, and it adds flavor. This is the calling of the Christian in the world.

2. We are not the source of our light. Rather, we reflect the light of Jesus Christ. All of our acts done in faith are not meant to bring us glory, but rather to point to Christ who is our light.

CONNECT

Read aloud Psalm 32:1–7.

1. Although we are tempted to "save face" in every situation, even when we are clearly in the wrong, we can relate to the psalmist's distress in verses 3–4, and we see in verse 5 that the poor in spirit are the ones who will be blessed.

2. Refer back to your answers in the "Focus" section. Check to see if forgiveness is at the core of your understanding of being blessed by God.

3. Answers will vary.

VISION

Discuss how you can apply what you have learned during the coming week. Close your study with prayer, giving thanks for God's great blessings.

Session 2

HEY DIDDLE, DIDDLE; EVERY JOT AND TITTLE!

FOCUS

The opening illustration reminds us of the many wrong turns and dead ends we reach in life. Ask for personal examples of how this is true in the lives of members of your group.

INFORM

Have a volunteer read aloud Matthew 5:17–20.

1. The Law will not be revoked until it has fully served its purpose. Those who wish to enter into heaven thinking Jesus has thrown out the Law will be grossly mistaken.

2. Those who can't keep the Law will be least in God's kingdom.

3. Jesus gives no hope at all for entering heaven by one's own righteousness.

4. Jesus did not come to abolish the Law. Rather, He came to fulfill it for us. Through faith, Jesus' perfect life is given to us, and therefore we are seen as holy in God's eyes.

CONNECT

1. Have participants place an *X* on the appropriate place on the scale that best describes how they feel. Answers will vary.

Read aloud John 19:16–22, 28–30.

2. Our holiness does not come through our own acts, but solely through faith in Christ's holy acts. It is difficult to see ourselves as holy people. Faith, however, enables us to see ourselves as God declares us!

VISION

Close your study with prayer, and close your prayers with this petition: "Lord Jesus, I thank You for fulfilling all righteousness for me on the cross and for making me holy. By Your Holy Spirit, may I live a life that mirrors Your righteous life."

Session 3
MURDER HE RE-WROTE

FOCUS

Ask participants to write their own definition of what murder is. Answers will vary.

INFORM

Have a volunteer read aloud Matthew 5:21–26.

1. Jesus teaches us that we can kill with words and thoughts just as easily as we can with a weapon.

2. The consequences of murder are judgment and hell. Jesus paid this penalty for us on the cross.

3. God has reconciled us to Himself through Jesus. He desires, in turn, that we be reconciled to one another.

Have someone read 1 John 3:11–16.

1. St. John refers to the very first murder in Genesis 4, where Cain killed his brother Abel. Cain killed his brother out of jealousy and hatred, because Abel gave the more acceptable offering to God.

2. Hating our brother or sister is killing them in our hearts. The God of love calls us to love.

3. As Jesus laid down His life for us, so we live sacrificial lives for one another.

CONNECT

Have volunteers read aloud Matthew 18:15–20.

1. Jesus outlines for us a practical and pleasing method of reconciliation. Instead of gossiping about another's actions or reporting him or her to someone else, we begin reconciliation by confronting the person directly. We do so with the motive of winning our brother or sister over.

2. Answers will vary.

3. Answers will vary.

4. Have participants look back at their definitions in the "Focus" section. Have them adapt or completely rewrite their definitions of *murder*.

VISION

Close your study with prayer, allowing time for silent prayer in which each participant can lift up the name of someone with whom she or he needs reconciliation.

Session 4

HOLY VOW! KEEPING YOUR WORD AND BEING FAITHFUL

FOCUS

Read aloud the opening paragraph. Answers will vary for both questions.

INFORM

Ask a volunteer to read aloud Matthew 5:27–32.

1. Jesus once again points out the full meaning of the Law. Adultery begins with lust in the heart.

2. Jesus teaches us to cut out any temptation that would lead us to sin.

3. Marriage is a gift from God. Those who enjoy this gift are called to keep it sacred.

4. Although God desires that no one get divorced, He does allow couples to divorce when a spouse is unfaithful. When adultery has been committed, the marriage vows have been broken. Even then, God's first desire is reconciliation.

Ask someone to read aloud Matthew 5:33–37.

1. God takes His Word seriously. By His Word He created the heavens and the earth. For our salvation, He sent His Son, the Word of life. We are called to keep our word pure, and the chief example of this is our marriage oath.

2. When we keep our word, there is no need to swear an oath to convince others that we are speaking the truth. For the Christian, we only swear by God's name in a court of law.

CONNECT

Ask volunteers to read aloud Romans 6:1–14.

1. Christ died for all of our sins, and these include the private sins of lust and shame. God comforts us with full and free forgiveness for all the sins of our past.

2. Through our Baptism, we have been made a new creation. Our calling is to daily fight our old nature and to flee temptation.

VISION

Close your study with prayer, giving particular thanks that God keeps His promises of love, mercy, and forgiveness to you!

Session 5

WHAT AN EXTRAORDINARY LOVE!

FOCUS

Read aloud or invite volunteers to read aloud the opening paragraphs. Then answer the questions that follow. Answers to the questions will vary.

INFORM

Read aloud Matthew 5:38–42.

1. Jesus tells His followers that if someone strikes you on the right cheek, you should turn to her or him the left. Jesus teaches that if someone wants to sue you and take your tunic, you should let him also have your cloak. Finally, Jesus tells His followers that if someone forces you to go one mile, you should go two miles.

2. Answers will vary. Ask participants to share the reasons for their answers.

3. We are to give to those in need. When we give to someone in need, we demonstrate God's love to that person.

Read aloud Matthew 5:43–48.

1. Jesus desires that we love our enemies. God loved us while we were still His enemies. In His love for us, God sent His only Son into this world to suffer and to die for our sins.

2. God cares and provides for His enemies.

3. God's love is extraordinary in that He loves all people and empowers us to love our enemies. It is not difficult to love those who demonstrate love to us. This is how the world loves. The real test of faith is to love those who don't love us.

4. Jesus teaches us to be perfect as our heavenly Father is perfect. In fact, Jesus teaches us to be like God in what we say and what we do. In reading verse 48 we become painfully aware of our imperfection and need for a Savior. In His love God sent His Son to suffer and to die on the cross for our imperfection. Jesus' blood covers our imperfection, making us holy.

Read aloud Romans 12:9–21.

1. Sincere love hates what is evil, clings to what is good, demonstrates devotion to one another, honors others above self, shares with people who are in need, practices hospitality, rejoices with those who rejoice, mourns with those who mourn, and lives in harmony with others.

2. Verse 18 tells us to live at peace with everyone. The disciple fosters peace and harmony with others. The responsibility for peace rests on the shoulders of the person of faith.

3. God will judge evil. A Christian's responsibility is to demonstrate the love of God in Christ Jesus to others.

4. The good that we have received by God's grace through faith in Jesus empowers us to demonstrate good to others.

CONNECT

Read aloud the opening paragraphs. Then invite a volunteer to read aloud Luke 23:32–34. Emphasize that as Jesus died on the cross, He prayed that the people who crucified Him would receive God's forgiveness. What wondrous and extraordinary love this is! Answers to all three questions in this section will vary.

VISION

Close by confessing your sinful inability to love those who hate you. Praise God for the forgiveness His Son won for you on the cross. Pray that the Holy Spirit would enable you to love those who don't demonstrate love to you and in so doing enable you to witness the power of God's love in Christ to them.

Session 6

HYPOCRITE!

FOCUS

Read aloud or invite a volunteer to read aloud the opening paragraphs. Then discuss the questions that follow.

1. Answers will vary. Some professions that commonly have a reputation for hypocrisy include lawyers, car salespersons, and real estate agents. Point out that many individuals who work in these professions are honest.

2. Answers will vary.

INFORM

Read aloud the opening paragraph. Then invite a volunteer to read aloud Matthew 6:1–4.

1. Selfish pride often motivates people to do "acts of righteousness" to be seen by men. These so-called acts of righteousness are done not to help others, but to build up and draw attention to the one who is doing the acts.

2. Jesus denounces those who tell everyone about their greatness as they give to others in need.

3. People who give by not letting their left hand know what the right hand is doing are motivated purely by their love for others.

Read aloud Matthew 6:5–8.

1. Hypocrites pray "standing in the synagogues and on the street corners to be seen by men." Pagans babble as they pray.

2. Jesus urges us to "go into your room, close the door and pray to your Father, who is unseen."

3. Jesus tells us that our Father in heaven knows what we need before we ask Him.

Read aloud or invite a volunteer to read aloud Matthew 6:16–18.

1. Jesus uses the phrase "I tell you the truth" to emphasize what He is about to say. "I tell you the truth" prompts the listener to tune into the message Jesus is about to share. Notice that Jesus uses this phrase to describe those who demonstrate an improper, self-centered motivation. "They have received their reward in full" implies that their reward is a temporary recognition from people, but that they will miss out on God's long-lasting blessings both while on earth and in eternity.

2. Once again, Jesus tells us to do that which will not draw attention to our good deeds. The hypocrites draw attention to their fasting by demonstrating how miserable they are. This simply draws attention to their good deeds. They are motivated by a self-centered desire to be noticed.

3. God the Father knows the motivation for all of our words and actions. We do

that which God desires as we are motivated by His love for us in Christ Jesus, not by our self-centered desire to gain attention. We will be rewarded by the salvation that Christ has won for us on the cross.

CONNECT

Invite a different volunteer to read aloud each of the woes included in Matthew 23:13, 15, 16, 23, 25, 27, and 29.

1. Verse 13—The Pharisees' teachings "lead people away" from God. Verse 15—The Pharisees' teachings "lead to hell." Verse 16—The Pharisees "make up rules" that lead people away from the truth. Verse 23—The Pharisees "neglect the important." Verse 25—The Pharisees' righteousness is only "outward not inward." Verse 27—The Pharisees appear "righteous" on the outside, but they are "corrupt" on the inside. Verse 29—The Pharisees "misrepresent their righteousness" and lie about their intentions. All of the woes point to the hypocrisy of those who misrepresent God and His teachings.

2. Answers will vary.

3. Answers will vary.

Read aloud Romans 7:21–25a.

1. Answers will vary.

2. Jesus did what He said He would do. He lived a perfect life to fulfill that which we were unable to do because of sin. Then He willingly suffered and died on the cross to receive the punishment we deserved. We receive the forgiveness of sins and eternal life through faith. Jesus rescued us from our bodies of death by dying in our place.

VISION

Read aloud this section. Close with a prayer asking that God's love in Christ would empower you to improve in the areas of your life where you have a tendency to demonstrate hypocrisy.

Session 7
LET US PRAY

FOCUS

Read aloud the opening paragraph. Then discuss the questions that follow. Answers will vary to both the questions.

INFORM

Read aloud or invite a volunteer to read aloud Matthew 6:9–13.

1. Jesus teaches us to address God as "Our Father." Jesus instructs us to "hallow," or to keep holy, the name of our Father in heaven.

2. We pray for the fulfillment of that which has come and will be completed on the final day—His kingdom in heaven and on earth.

3. We pray confidently that God will provide for all of our needs.

4. We pray for forgiveness and the power to forgive those who sin against us. We also pray that God would keep us from giving in to temptation and deliver us from the power of Satan.

Read aloud or invite a volunteer to read aloud Matthew 6:14–15.

1. The forgiveness that Jesus won for us on the cross motivates and empowers us to forgive those who sin against us.

2. God's love in Christ motivates us to forgive others. We can never earn God's forgiveness. But thanks be to God, He sent His only Son to win for us forgiveness of sins and eternal life by His death on the cross. Remind participants that we need to use Scripture to interpret Scripture. All of Scripture points to the central teaching of justification by grace through faith, summarized in Ephesians 2:8–9, "For it is by grace you have been saved, through faith—and this not from yourselves, it is the gift of God—not by works, so that no one can boast."

CONNECT

1. Answers will vary.

2. Through His death on the cross, Jesus won for us full and complete access to the Father. By His grace through faith we can draw near to God. God is always faithful to His promises.

3. The Holy Spirit testifies with our spirit. The Spirit intercedes for us when we do not know what to pray for.

VISION

Read aloud the closing paragraphs. Then pray together the Lord's Prayer.

Session 8

SHOW ME THE TREASURE!

FOCUS

Read aloud the opening paragraph. Then direct participants to select the top five things they would take. Tell them they have 30 seconds to make their lists. Answers will vary. Have participants explain the reasons for their answers.

INFORM

Read aloud Jesus' instructions on the use of our treasures in Matthew 6:19–24.

1. Earthly treasures are those that will ultimately disappear. Heavenly treasures are those that will endure for eternity.

2. Anything that is number one in our life is our treasure. If our pursuit of wealth is our number one goal in life, then God will become number two. The First Commandment reminds us, "You shall have no other gods." Anytime we make anyone or anything other than God Himself number one in our life, we break the First Commandment.

3. Ultimately, that which we pursue becomes the most important thing in our life. Often we may not realize it when we fill our body with darkness. When we pursue anyone or anything other than God, we begin to crowd God out of our life.

4. Verse 24 states, "No one can serve two masters." That which becomes the most important thing—number one in your life—becomes your master.

Read aloud the paragraph. Then invite a volunteer to read aloud Revelation 3:14–18.

1. Their spirituality is described as lukewarm. They are neither hot or cold.

2. They have deceived themselves into believing that if they are rich, they do not need a thing. Unfortunately, their pursuit of riches has left them spiritually bankrupt.

3. God counsels the church at Laodicea to find their wealth in Him alone. The gold, white clothes, and salve refer to the three things the Laodiceans take great pride in: financial wealth, an extensive textile industry, and a famous eye salve. Note how God uses these earthly items as symbols of what He would have us seek from Him—heavenly riches, forgiveness, and eyes that see the truth. God tells the people to replace their pursuit of earthly wealth with a pursuit of that which will have eternal consequences—faith in Jesus Christ crucified.

CONNECT

Read aloud the opening paragraph. Then invite a volunteer to read aloud 1 Timothy 6:17–19.

1. Answers will vary.

2. We are rich in Christ, for through faith in Him we receive the riches of heaven.

3. Motivated by the riches that God has bestowed on us through faith in Jesus, we share our wealth with others. His love for us empowers us to do good toward others.

VISION

Read aloud the closing paragraphs. Then pray that, empowered by the Holy Spirit, you will keep God number one in your life and that you will share with others the earthly treasures He has provided you.

Session 9

STRESS LESS!

FOCUS

Read aloud the opening paragraph. Then direct participants to complete the two questions. Answers will vary.

INFORM

Read aloud the opening paragraph. Then invite a volunteer to read aloud Matthew 6:25–34.

1. Verse 25: Life is more important than food, and the body is more important than clothes.

2. Verse 26: Your Father in heaven feeds even the birds.

3. Verse 27: You cannot add a single hour to your life by worrying.

4. Verses 28–30: God clothes even the grass of the field. He will clothe you also.

5. Verses 31–32: Your heavenly Father knows what you need and will provide it.

6. Verse 33: Seek first God's kingdom, and all the things you need will be provided.

7. Verse 34: Do not worry about tomorrow, for tomorrow will worry about itself.

Invite volunteers to read aloud Jesus' send-off speech to the disciples in Matthew 10:5–30.

1. Jesus tells His disciples to take nothing for their journey. They will receive their provisions from the people with whom they share His message of love and forgiveness. In faith the disciples journey, trusting that God will provide all they need to sustain their lives.

2. Jesus assures His disciples that they will be given the words to say. They do not have to worry about having the right words.

3. God promises to protect His disciples from dangers. He will be with them always.

CONNECT

Read aloud the opening paragraph. Then invite a volunteer to read aloud Philippians 4:6—8.

1. Answers will vary.

2. Answers will vary. Empowered by God's love for us in Christ, our "thanksgiving list" can dwarf our "complaint list."

3. We can dwell on the great love God has demonstrated to us through His Son's death on the cross. Though we may face trials and tribulations in this world, we have received the gift of eternal life in heaven. Nothing can separate us from God's love in Christ Jesus.

VISION

Read aloud the closing paragraphs. Then pray together that you might be empowered to be thankful to God in all situations.

Session 10
A Visine Cure for Judging Others

FOCUS

Read aloud the opening paragraphs. The story will guide participants into the main concept explored in this session—judging others. Answers to the questions will vary.

INFORM

Read aloud Matthew 7:1–6.

1. Jesus warns us not to judge others. We will be judged in the same way we judge others.

2. Often as we judge others' sins, we fail to recognize and confess our own sins. We often overlook the enormity of our own sin as we focus on a sin of someone else.

3. Jesus tells us to stop sinning—take the plank out of our own eye—before we judge the sins of others.

Read aloud Romans 14:1–3, 7–13.

1. In "disputable matters"—matters in which God's Word is silent—we have freedom to choose.

2. God alone can judge our actions and the motivation for them.

3. Christ alone is the judge of both the living and the dead. Jesus will judge us righteous through faith. Jesus will condemn those who do not possess saving faith in Him.

4. Paul admonishes us to stop judging others. Instead, he tells us not to put any stumbling block—something that causes a person to fall into sin—in the way of our brother.

CONNECT

Read aloud the opening paragraph.

1. Answers will vary.

2. Answers will vary.

3. As we confess that we are the chief of sinners for whom Jesus died, we are able to put another person's sin into its proper perspective. Jesus desires that we judge other's actions realizing that our own sin led Him to the cross to suffer and to die.

VISION

Read aloud the closing paragraph. Close by confessing your sinfulness and by giving thanks to God for the forgiveness Jesus won for you on the cross. Then ask that God would enable you to speak the truth in love to those who are caught in the struggle of sin, to step out of judgment, and to receive the assurance of God's grace through faith in Jesus.

Session 11
FOLLOW THE NARROW BRICK ROAD

FOCUS

Read aloud the opening paragraph. Then invite a volunteer to read aloud the lines from "The Road Less Traveled." Then discuss the questions that follow. Answers will vary.

INFORM

Read aloud or invite a volunteer to read aloud Matthew 7:7–14.

1. Jesus promises, "For everyone who asks receives; he who seeks finds; and to him who knocks, the door will be opened."

2. Our earthly parents provide for our needs. So too will our heavenly Father provide all that we need to sustain this life.

3. Answers will vary. We are to act and speak to others as we would want them to act and speak to us.

4. The road that leads to destruction is broad and the gate is wide. The road that leads to life is narrow and the gate is small.

Read aloud John 10:7–10.

1. Jesus calls Himself "the gate for the sheep."

2. All who enter through Him will be saved. Jesus provides life.

CONNECT

Read aloud the opening paragraph. Then invite a volunteer to read aloud Proverbs 3:5–6.

1. Answers will vary.

2. Answers will vary. Most will admit that at times they fail to seek direction for their lives from God's Word.

3. Answers will vary.

VISION

Read aloud the closing paragraphs of this session. Pray together that, empowered by the Spirit, you would ask, seek, and knock, confident that God will provide for all of your needs—both great and small.

Session 12

WHY DO WE KEEP FOOLING AROUND?

FOCUS

Urge participants to complete the two acrostics—one describing wisdom and the other describing foolishness. Provide time for participants to share their acrostics.

INFORM

Read aloud or invite a volunteer to read aloud Matthew 7:15–28.

1. False prophets come in sheep's clothing. You can tell them by their fruit—what they say and what they do.

2. Only those who possess saving faith in Jesus will receive eternal life. Not everyone who calls, "Lord, Lord," possesses saving faith. The false prophets lack faith in Jesus. They may say the right words and do the right actions, but without faith they will receive only eternal death.

3. A wise person hears Jesus' words and puts them into practice. Empowered by God's Word and the message of salvation through Jesus Christ found in the Word, a wise person has the foundation that will enable him or her to endure temptations in this world and provide the greatest prize—eternal life in heaven. Built upon the foundation of faith in Christ Jesus, we can endure all.

4. Answers will vary. Foolish people often build their lives upon material things or sinful pleasures.

5. The crowds were amazed at Jesus' teachings.

Read aloud Acts 4:5–12.

1. They healed the crippled man by the authority given to them by Jesus Christ.

2. Peter describes Jesus as "the stone you builders rejected, which has become the capstone." Jesus is the foundation upon which we receive salvation. Salvation is found in no one else.

CONNECT

Read aloud the opening paragraph. Then invite volunteers to read aloud Proverbs 4:1–9.

1. Answers will vary. At times it is very difficult to distinguish between wisdom and foolishness.

2. Answers will vary. The most important thing we can find is wisdom; wisdom is found in no one other than Jesus Christ. Nothing else really matters in life, because the gift that Jesus provides through faith is the only gift we will take with us from this life into eternity.

3. Answers will vary.

4. Answers will vary.

VISION

Read aloud the closing paragraphs. Then pray that God would provide you wisdom —wisdom found only through faith in Jesus—as you face day-to-day life situations, as you experience joys and sorrows, and as you face death.

www.ingramcontent.com/pod-product-compliance
Lightning Source LLC
Chambersburg PA
CBHW081525040426
42447CB00013B/3343